Learn to Wr: Sentences

Summer Vacation

The Danger Twins Writing Series

ISBN PAPERBACK: 978-1-956547-11-5

Names, characters, places, and incidents are the product of the author's imagination
or are used fictitiously. Any resemblance to actual persons, living or dead, events, or
locales is entirely coincidental.

Book design by Anne Lusher

Published by Unplanned Books, LLC.

UNPLANNED BOOKS

Reading and
writing
with the
Danger Twins

THE DANGER TWINS

Let's work together to

create a few new and

colorful sentences.

Your friends,

Alaina & Sean

*Trace the pronouns below. Then, choose one of
the three pronouns and write it next to the arrow.*

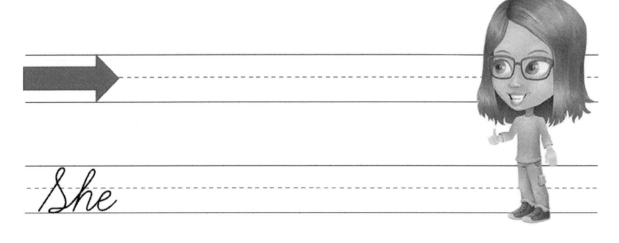

➡

She

She   She   She

He

He   He   He

They

They   They   They

Trace the words below. Then, choose one of
the three words and write it next to the arrow.

STEP
TWO

⮕ -

should

should   should   should

would

would   would   would

could

could   could   could

Trace the word pairs below. Then, choose one of the three word pairs and write it next to the arrow

STEP THREE

have seen

have seen   have seen

have observed

have observed have observed

not see

not see   not see   not see

6

Trace the number words below. Then, choose one of the three numbers and write it next to the arrow.

STEP FOUR

⟹ ....

two

two   *two*   *two*

three

three   *three*   *three*

five

five   *five*   *five*

7

Trace the color names below. Then, choose one color and write the word next to the arrow.

STEP
FIVE

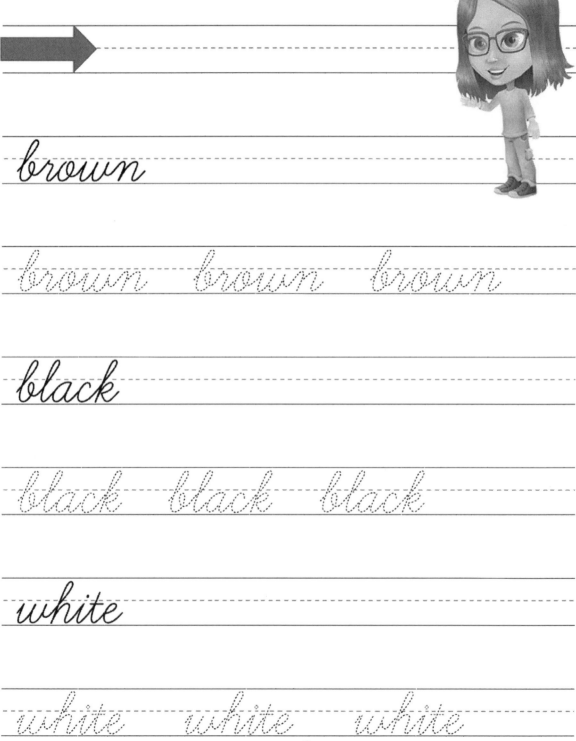

brown

brown   brown   brown

black

black   black   black

white

white   white   white

8

Trace the animal names below. Then, choose one animal and write the word next to the arrow.

STEP SIX

➡️

dogs

dogs   dogs   dogs

goats

goats   goats   goats

cats

cats   cats   cats

9

Trace the location descriptors below. Then, choose one and write it next to the arrow.

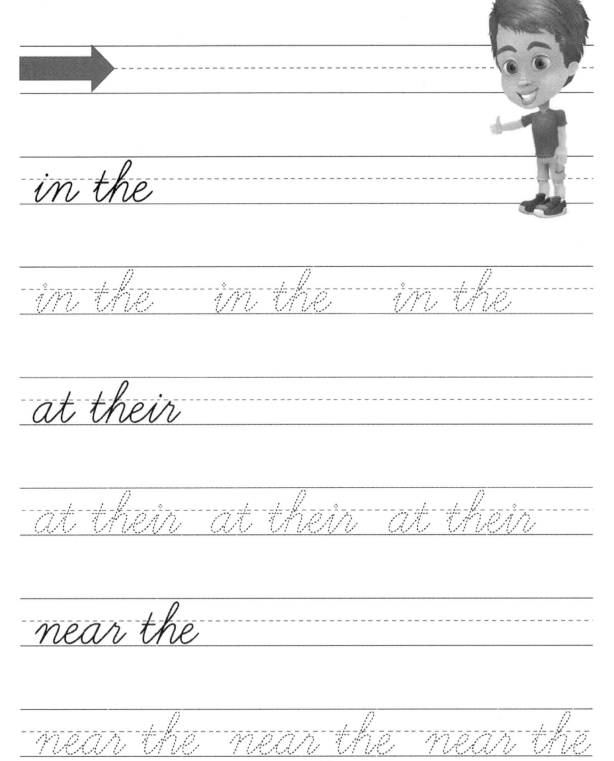

in the

in the   in the   in the

at their

at their   at their   at their

near the

near the   near the   near the

10

Trace the adjectives below. Then, choose one adjective and write it next to the arrow.

STEP EIGHT

➡️

tiny

tiny   tiny   tiny

small

small   small   small

large

large   large   large

Trace the adjectives below. Then, choose one
adjective and write it next to the arrow.

→

antique

antique   antique

rustic

rustic   rustic   rustic

old

old   old   old

12

Trace the color names below. Then, choose one color and write the word next to the arrow.

STEP TEN

red

red   red   red

tan

tan   tan   tan

yellow

yellow   yellow   yellow

Trace the building names below. Then, choose one building and write the word next to the arrow.

farm house.

farm house   farm house

barn.

barn   barn   barn

cottage.

cottage   cottage   cottage

Trace the completed sentences below.
Go back and read the words after each arrow.
Read them in order, just like the sentences below.

She should have seen

three brown goats in the

small rustic red barn.

He could not see two

black cats at their tiny

old yellow cottage.

Go back to Steps 1-11 and select different words and write new sentences below.

Go back to Steps 1–11 and select different words and write new sentences below.

NEW
SENTENCE

Go back to Steps 1–11 and select different words and write new sentences below.

NEW SENTENCE

Think about the summer, and then write down a word for each letter of the alphabet.

A a

B b

C c

D d

E e

F f

BONUS WORDS FROM THE DANGER TWINS

Think about the summer, and then
write down a word
for each letter of the alphabet.

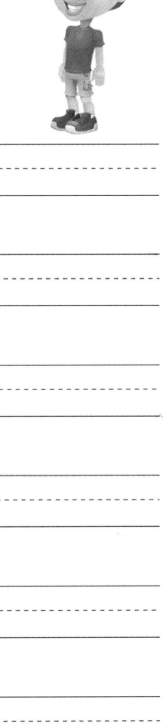

G g

H h

I i

J j

K k

L l

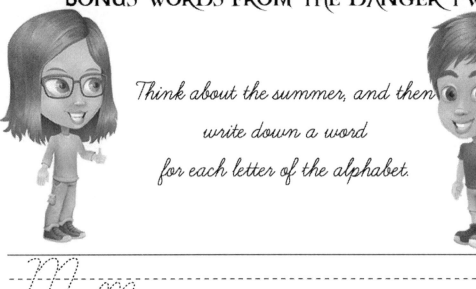

Think about the summer, and then write down a word for each letter of the alphabet.

M m

N n

O o

P p

Q q

R r

Think about the summer, and then write down a word for each letter of the alphabet.

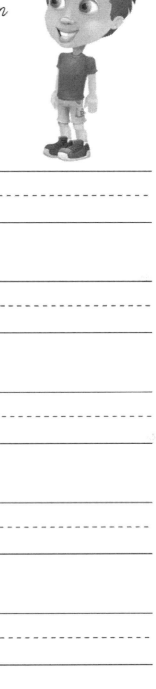

Ss

Tt

Uu

Vv

Ww

Zz

a a a a a

a a a a a

a a a a a

a a a a a

adventure

adventure

Write a quick story about
a summer adventure.

Practice tracing and writing
the letters in cursive.

𝒶

a a a a a

a a a a a a

a a a a a

a a a a a

apple

apple

Write a quick story about
an apple orchard.

Practice tracing and writing
the letters in cursive.

B

B B B B B

b b b b b b

B B B B B

b b b b b b

barefoot

barefoot

Write a quick story about walking barefoot.

B

B B B B B

b b b b b b

B B B B B

b b b b b b

barbeque

barbeque

Write a quick story about attending a barbeque.

Practice tracing and writing
the letters in cursive.

C

C C C C C

C C C C C C

C C C C C

C C C C C C

camping

camping

Write a quick story about camping in the woods.

C

Practice tracing and writing
the letters in cursive.

C

c c c c c

c c c c c c

C C C C C

c c c c c c

celebration

celebration

Write a quick story about a summer celebration.

C

Practice tracing and writing
the letters in cursive.

$\mathcal{D}$

$\mathcal{D}$ $\mathcal{D}$ $\mathcal{D}$ $\mathcal{D}$ $\mathcal{D}$ $\mathcal{D}$

d d d d d d

$\mathcal{D}$ $\mathcal{D}$ $\mathcal{D}$ $\mathcal{D}$ $\mathcal{D}$

d d d d d d

dandelions

dandelions

Write a quick story about dandelions.

Practice tracing and writing the letters in cursive.

Ɛ Ɛ Ɛ Ɛ Ɛ

e e e e e e

Ɛ Ɛ Ɛ Ɛ Ɛ

e e e e e e

explore

explore

Write a quick story about where you like to explore.

e

Practice tracing and writing
the letters in cursive.

$\mathcal{F}$

$\mathcal{F}$ $\mathcal{F}$ $\mathcal{F}$ $\mathcal{F}$ $\mathcal{F}$

f f f f f f

$\mathcal{F}$ $\mathcal{F}$ $\mathcal{F}$ $\mathcal{F}$ $\mathcal{F}$

f f f f f f

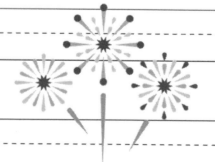

fireworks

fireworks

Write a quick story about seeing fireworks in the sky.

f

Practice tracing and writing

the letters in cursive.

$\mathcal{F}$ $\mathcal{F}$ $\mathcal{F}$ $\mathcal{F}$ $\mathcal{F}$

f f f f f f

$\mathcal{F}$ $\mathcal{F}$ $\mathcal{F}$ $\mathcal{F}$ $\mathcal{F}$

f f f f f f

farm

farm

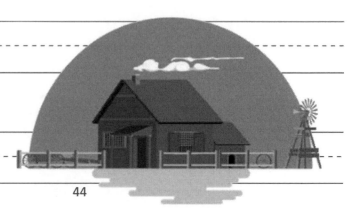

44

Write a quick story about visiting a farm.

𝒢

𝓖 𝓖 𝓖 𝓖 𝓖

𝑔 𝑔 𝑔 𝑔 𝑔 𝑔

𝒢 𝒢 𝒢 𝒢 𝒢

𝑔 𝑔 𝑔 𝑔 𝑔 𝑔

garden

garden

Write a quick story about
working in a garden.

Practice tracing and writing the letters in cursive.

H

H H H H H

h h h h h h

H H H H H

h h h h h h

heat

heat

Write a quick story about the summer heat.

H H H H H

h h h h h h

H H H H H

h h h h h h

holidays

holidays

*Write a quick story about
the summer holidays.*

Practice tracing and writing
the letters in cursive.

I I I I I

i i i i i

I I I I I

i i i i i i

ice cream

ice cream

Write a quick story about eating ice cream.

Practice tracing and writing
the letters in cursive.

J J J J J

j j j j j j

J J J J J

j j j j j j

July

July

JULY						
MO	TU	WE	TH	FR	SA	SU
		1	2	3	4	5
6	7	8	9	10	11	12
13	14	15	16	17	18	19
20	21	22	23	24	25	26
27	28	29	30	31		

Write a quick story about
what you did in July.

K

K K K K K K

k k k k k k

K K K K K

k k k k k k

kite

kite

Write a quick story about flying a kite.

$\mathscr{L} \quad \mathscr{L} \quad \mathscr{L} \quad \mathscr{L} \quad \mathscr{L}$

$l \quad l \quad l \quad l \quad l \quad l$

$\mathscr{L} \quad \mathscr{L} \quad \mathscr{L} \quad \mathscr{L} \quad \mathscr{L}$

$l \quad l \quad l \quad l \quad l \quad l$

lemonade

lemonade

Write a quick story about drinking lemonade.

Practice tracing and writing
the letters in cursive.

L

L L L L L

l l l l l l

L L L L L

l l l l l l

lifeguard

lifeguard

Write a quick story about the role of a lifeguard.

ℳ ℳ ℳ ℳ ℳ

m m m m m m

ℳ ℳ ℳ ℳ ℳ

m m m m m m

memories

memories

Write a quick story about your best summer memories.

n n n n n

n n n n n n

n n n n n

n n n n n n

nap

nap

Write a quick story about
taking a nap outside.

$\mathcal{O}$ $\mathcal{O}$ $\mathcal{O}$ $\mathcal{O}$ $\mathcal{O}$

o o o o o o

$\mathcal{O}$ $\mathcal{O}$ $\mathcal{O}$ $\mathcal{O}$ $\mathcal{O}$

o o o o o o

outdoors

outdoors

Write a quick story about spending playtime outdoors.

Practice tracing and writing

the letters in cursive.

O O O O O

O O O O O O

O O O O O

O O O O O O

ocean

ocean

Write a quick story about spending time in the ocean.

Practice tracing and writing

the letters in cursive.

p

p p p p p

p p p p p p

p p p p p

p p p p p p

picnic

picnic

Write a quick story about having a picnic.

p

p p p p p

p p p p p p

p p p p p

p p p p p p

popsicle

popsicle

Write a quick story about your favorite flavor of popsicle.

Practice tracing and writing
the letters in cursive.

$\mathcal{Q}$

$\mathcal{Q}$ $\mathcal{Q}$ $\mathcal{Q}$ $\mathcal{Q}$ $\mathcal{Q}$

q q q q q q

$\mathcal{Q}$ $\mathcal{Q}$ $\mathcal{Q}$ $\mathcal{Q}$ $\mathcal{Q}$

q q q q q q

quiet

quiet

Write a quick story about being quiet in the woods.

Practice tracing and writing the letters in cursive.

R

R R R R R

r r r r r r

R R R R R

r r r r r r

ripe

ripe

Write a quick story about tasting fresh, ripe fruit.

Practice tracing and writing

the letters in cursive.

R R R R R

r r r r r r

R R R R R

r r r r r r

road trip

road trip

Write a quick story about a summer road trip.

S S S S S

ʃ ʃ ʃ ʃ ʃ ʃ

S S S S S

ʃ ʃ ʃ ʃ ʃ ʃ

sunburn

sunburn

Write a quick story about a sunburn.

$\mathcal{S}$ $\mathcal{S}$ $\mathcal{S}$ $\mathcal{S}$ $\mathcal{S}$

swimming

swimming

Write a quick story about visiting a pool and swimming.

Practice tracing and writing

the letters in cursive.

$\mathcal{T}$

$\mathcal{T}$ $\mathcal{T}$ $\mathcal{T}$ $\mathcal{T}$ $\mathcal{T}$

t t t t t t t

$\mathcal{T}$ $\mathcal{T}$ $\mathcal{T}$ $\mathcal{T}$ $\mathcal{T}$

t t t t t t

t-shirt

t-shirt

Write a quick story about wearing your best t-shirt.

t

U

U U U U U

u u u u u u

U U U U U

u u u u u u

unforgettable

unforgettable

Write a quick story about an unforgettable moment.

$\mathcal{V}$ $\mathcal{V}$ $\mathcal{V}$ $\mathcal{V}$ $\mathcal{V}$

u u u u u u

$\mathcal{V}$ $\mathcal{V}$ $\mathcal{V}$ $\mathcal{V}$ $\mathcal{V}$

u u u u u u

visit

visit

Write a quick story about who you went to visit.

$\mathcal{V}$ $\mathcal{V}$ $\mathcal{V}$ $\mathcal{V}$ $\mathcal{V}$

u u u u u u u

$\mathcal{V}$ $\mathcal{V}$ $\mathcal{V}$ $\mathcal{V}$ $\mathcal{V}$

u u u u u u

vacation

vacation

Write a quick story about the best part of summer vacation.

Practice tracing and writing
the letters in cursive.

$\mathcal{W}$

$\mathcal{W}$ $\mathcal{W}$ $\mathcal{W}$ $\mathcal{W}$ $\mathcal{W}$

w w w w w w w

$\mathcal{W}$ $\mathcal{W}$ $\mathcal{W}$ $\mathcal{W}$ $\mathcal{W}$

w w w w w w

water

water

Write a quick story about
splashing in the water.

Practice tracing and writing

the letters in cursive.

X X X X X

x x x x x x

X X X X X

x x x x x x

relax

relax

Write a quick story about how you like to relax.

Practice tracing and writing
the letters in cursive.

𝒴 𝒴 𝒴 𝒴 𝒴

𝓎 𝓎 𝓎 𝓎 𝓎 𝓎

𝒴 𝒴 𝒴 𝒴 𝒴

𝓎 𝓎 𝓎 𝓎 𝓎 𝓎

yard

yard

Write a quick story about
working in your yard.

$\mathcal{Z}$

$\mathcal{Z}$ $\mathcal{Z}$ $\mathcal{Z}$ $\mathcal{Z}$ $\mathcal{Z}$

$\mathcal{g}$ $\mathcal{g}$ $\mathcal{g}$ $\mathcal{g}$ $\mathcal{g}$ $\mathcal{g}$

$\mathcal{Z}$ $\mathcal{Z}$ $\mathcal{Z}$ $\mathcal{Z}$ $\mathcal{Z}$

$\mathcal{g}$ $\mathcal{g}$ $\mathcal{g}$ $\mathcal{g}$ $\mathcal{g}$ $\mathcal{g}$

zoo

zoo

Write a quick story about visiting the zoo.

THE DANGER TWINS

theDangerTwins.com

Printed in Great Britain
by Amazon

86452072R00059